UNDERSTANDING VIRUSES

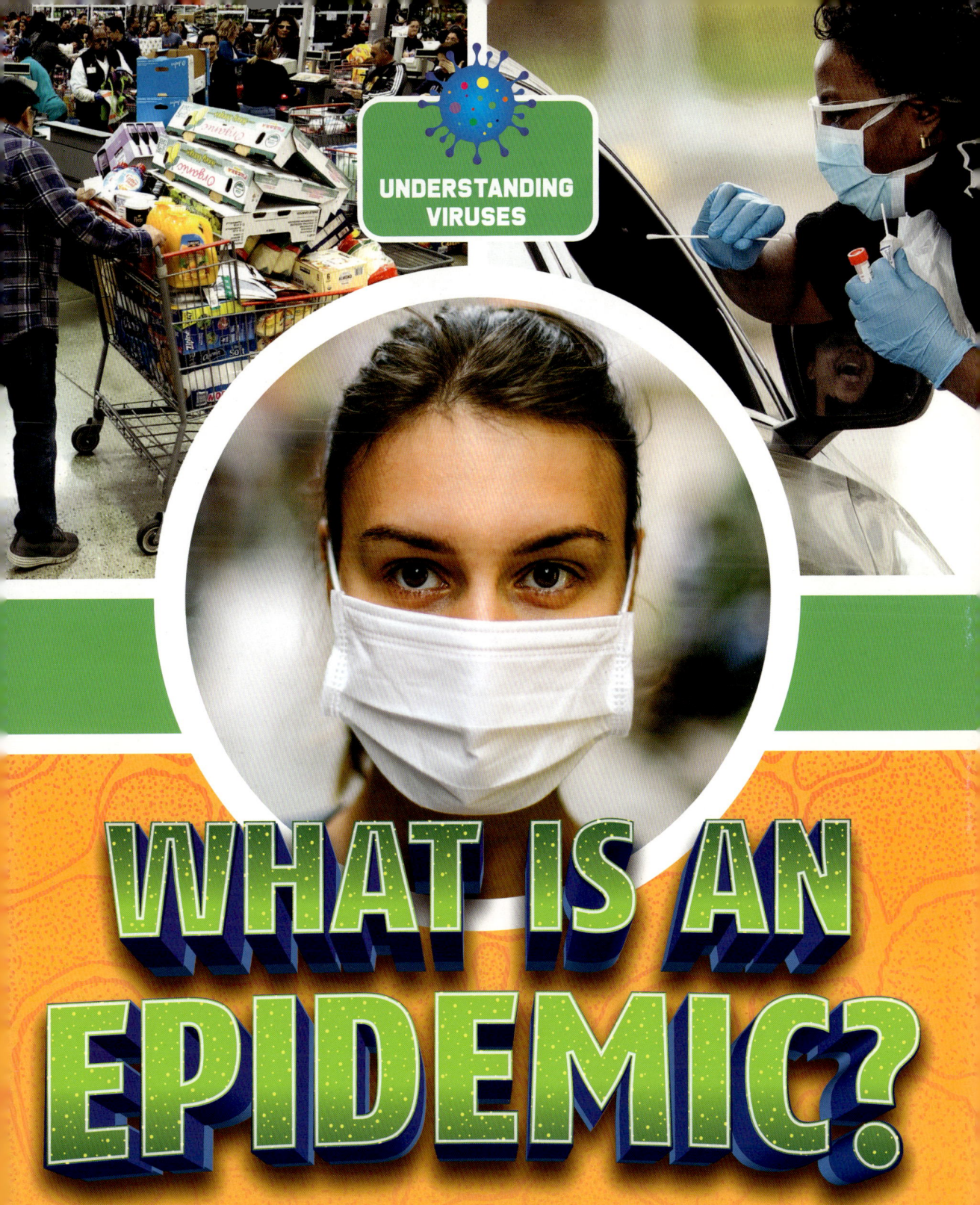

WHAT IS AN EPIDEMIC?

Heather C. Hudak

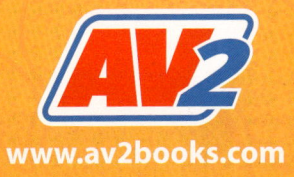

AV2

www.av2books.com

AV2

Step 1
Go to www.av2books.com

Step 2
Enter this unique code

NWMIFDFJ2

Step 3
Explore your interactive eBook!

CONTENTS
- 4 SARS Spreads
- 6 On the Brink
- 8 Strength in Numbers
- 10 Under Investigation
- 12 Faster and Farther
- 14 Working Together
- 16 Healthcare Heroes
- 18 Recent Epidemics
- 20 Raising Awareness
- 21 Activity: Make an Epidemic Kit
- 22 Epidemic Quiz

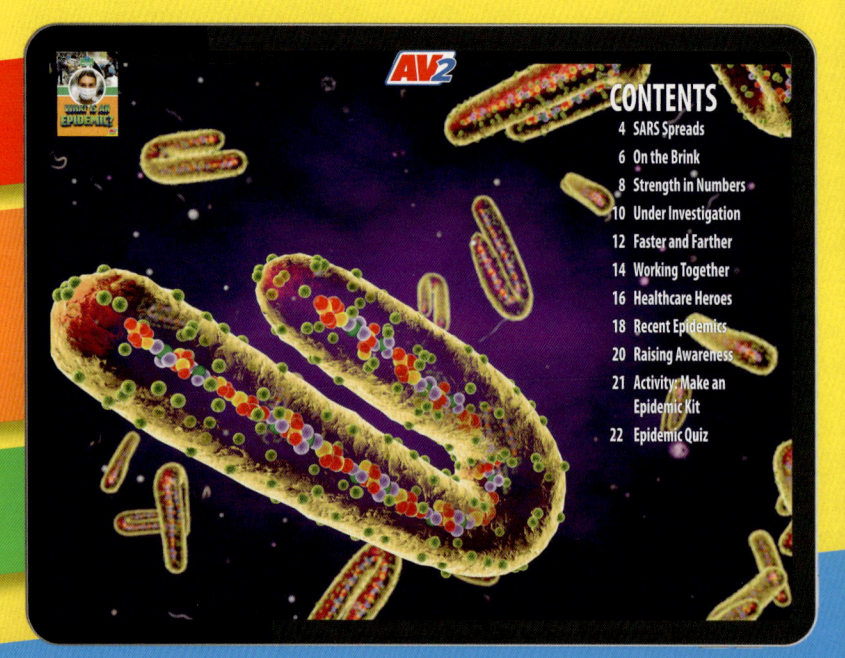

AV2 is optimized for use on any device

Your interactive eBook comes with...

Contents
Browse a live contents page to easily navigate through resources

Audio
Listen to sections of the book read aloud

Videos
Watch informative video clips

Weblinks
Gain additional information for research

Try This!
Complete activities and hands-on experiments

Key Words
Study vocabulary, and complete a matching word activity

Quizzes
Test your knowledge

Slideshows
View images and captions

... and much, much more!

2

View new titles and product videos at www.av2books.com

WHAT IS AN EPIDEMIC?

CONTENTS

SARS Spreads 4
On the Brink 6
Strength in Numbers 8
Under Investigation 10
Faster and Farther 12
Working Together 14
Healthcare Heroes 16
Recent Epidemics 18
Raising Awareness 20
Activity: Make an Epidemic Kit 21
Epidemic Quiz 22
Key Words/Index 23

SARS Spreads

In November 2002, a new type of **virus** spread throughout southern China. It caused a disease called SARS. No one knew where the virus had come from. Within a few months, hundreds of people were sick. Some of them died. In February 2003, a man from China went to Hong Kong on a trip. He did not know he had SARS. Other guests at the hotel where the man was staying caught the SARS virus from him. They took it back to their countries when they flew home.

SARS soon made its way to North America, South America, Europe, and other parts of Asia. It was an epidemic. Countries around the world prepared for many people to get sick. Scientists worked hard to learn more about SARS. They needed to stop the virus before it got out of control. People who became sick were **quarantined**. This kept them from spreading the virus to others. These quick responses by scientists and governments worked so well that SARS was under control by July 2003.

The first case of SARS was recorded in the city of Foshan, in the Chinese province of Guangdong.

FAST FACT

More than 8,000 people were infected with SARS. Nearly 800 died.

What Is an Epidemic? 5

On the Brink

A disease caused by a virus is called a viral disease. Scientists count how many people get different diseases each year. They compare the number of cases of each disease to past years. This is how they find out how many cases are normal for a certain time and place. Sometimes, the number is higher than normal. This is called an outbreak.

Some schools have emergency plans to prepare for possible disease outbreaks.

Imagine a classroom at school. One or two students may get a cold each week. This is normal. However, if 10 kids suddenly get a cold in the same week, it is an outbreak.

In rare cases, a disease may spread quickly to many people. It may start to appear in different communities, regions, or even countries all at once. This is more than just an outbreak. It is an epidemic. An epidemic can become a **pandemic** if the disease is not contained. A pandemic spreads to even more places than an epidemic and affects a large percentage of people around the world.

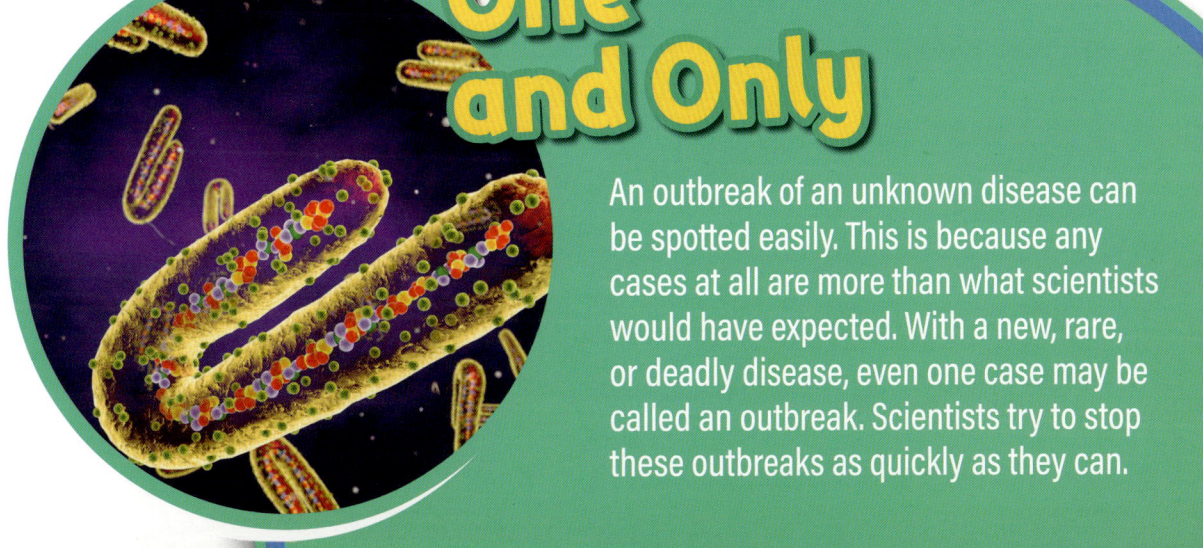

The World Health Organization (WHO) is an international institution that monitors outbreaks around the world.

One and Only

An outbreak of an unknown disease can be spotted easily. This is because any cases at all are more than what scientists would have expected. With a new, rare, or deadly disease, even one case may be called an outbreak. Scientists try to stop these outbreaks as quickly as they can.

Strength in Numbers

Doctors expect some outbreaks each year. For instance, they know many people will get sick with the flu. Sometimes, far more people get the flu than doctors expected. These cases may only happen in a certain community, state, or country. This is an outbreak. Even one or two cases of a virus can spread quickly and lead to an outbreak.

About 40,000 people in the United States get **human immunodeficiency virus (HIV)** each year. This is a large number. Still, it is a normal amount. There needs to be a sudden change in the level of cases for there to be an outbreak. By 2000, measles had almost disappeared in the United States. This means that even a small number of new cases of measles would be called an outbreak today. In 2019, there were about 1,200 cases of measles across the United States. This was an outbreak.

Most people who catch the flu recover completely in one or two weeks. Elderly people, infants, or those with chronic illnesses may experience complications.

Understanding Viruses

U.S. Flu Map

This map shows the development of the flu season in the United States at the beginning of 2020. Many states had more sick people than **average**.

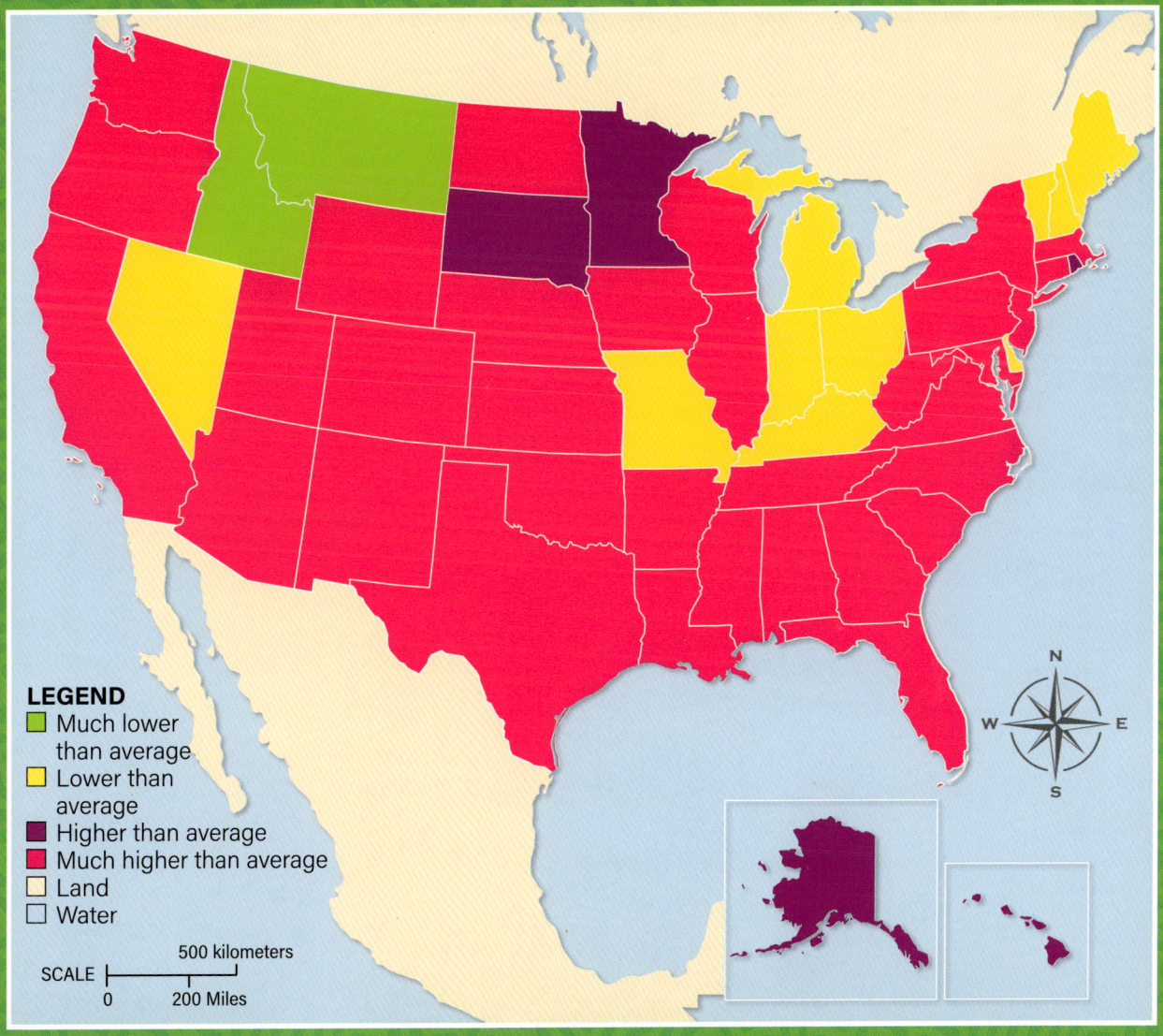

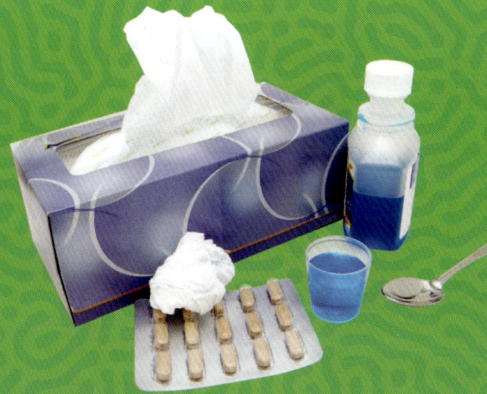

LEGEND
- Much lower than average
- Lower than average
- Higher than average
- Much higher than average
- Land
- Water

SCALE: 0 — 500 kilometers / 200 Miles

The period when most flu cases occur is known as flu season. Every year, flu season begins around October and continues until May.

What Is an Epidemic?

Under Investigation

Scientists begin to **investigate** outbreaks right away. They want to know how many people are **infected** with the virus. They try to find out where the virus came from. Scientists look for ways to stop the virus from spreading. They hope to keep others from getting sick. Their work will help stop future outbreaks, or worse, an epidemic.

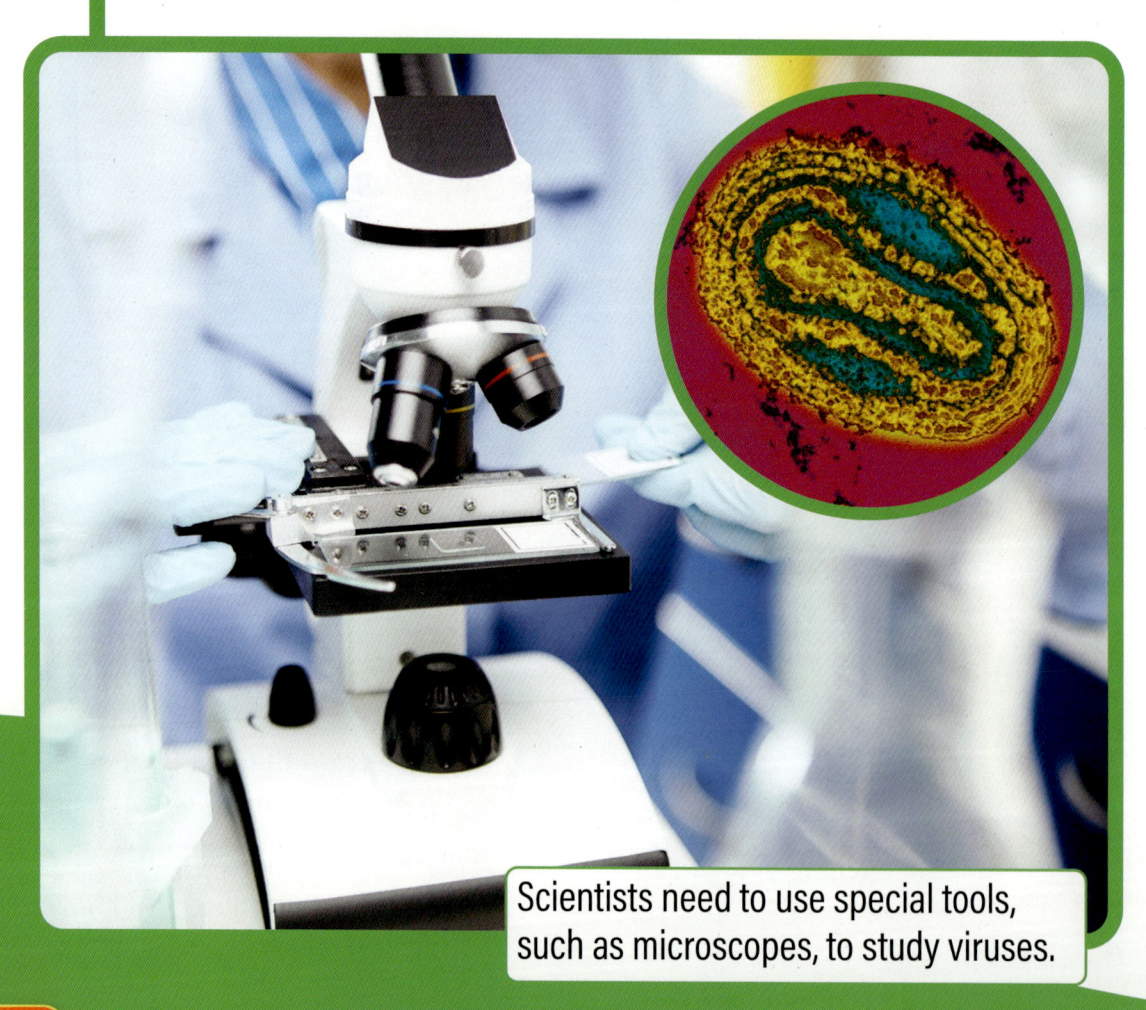

Scientists need to use special tools, such as microscopes, to study viruses.

Understanding Viruses

Outbreak Investigation Steps

There are many steps in an outbreak investigation.

STEP 1: Prepare to investigate
- Learn the facts about the virus

STEP 2: Is there an outbreak?
- Compare past data and new cases
- Talk to experts and health workers
- Decide if there really is an outbreak

STEP 3: Make sure the findings are accurate
- Look for even more data
- Do more tests
- Confirm the findings

STEP 4: What does a case look like?
- Figure out the virus's signs and **symptoms**
- Determine who has the virus

STEP 5: Record cases
- Collect the names and ages of each infected person, along with other details

STEP 6: What happened?
- Research what may have caused the virus to spread and how it can be stopped

STEP 7: Stop the spread
- Take action to stop the virus

STEP 8: Report
- Share findings with scientists, governments, health workers, and the **media**

Faster and Farther

Today, viruses spread faster than ever before. Airplanes are one of the main reasons for this increase in speed. Infected people can travel anywhere in the world in just a few hours. They may spread a disease to people who sit close by on the plane. Each of those people can then infect others, too. They might transfer to another plane and take the virus to other parts of the world. Ships, trains, and cars also help viruses spread quickly.

One of the most-used commercial airplanes can carry up to 180 passengers at a time.

In 2020, during the COVID-19 outbreak, about 700 passengers on the *Diamond Princess* cruise ship caught the virus while on board.

More people live in cities now than in the past. They live and work close together. This makes it easier for viruses to spread from person to person, or from contact with infected objects. Some people may never show symptoms of the virus. Still, they can spread it. A virus may spread to many places and infect a large number of people before scientists even know about it. This makes it harder for them to find out where it started.

Epidemics over the Years

This graph shows the number of new epidemics that took place each year between 2011 and 2017.

Year	Number of Epidemic Events around the World
2011	179
2012	183
2013	164
2014	197
2015	182
2016	213
2017	189

What Is an Epidemic?

Working Together

New viruses are always being discovered. It is important for scientists to study them. Their goal is to learn as much as possible about all kinds of viruses, and stop them from spreading. Scientists look at what causes them, where they come from, and how they spread. They also look at what has been done in the past to stop them.

As there are no **vaccines** or treatments for new viruses, health and science experts must act fast during an outbreak of a new virus. They need to quickly find ways to stop the virus and save lives. Experts share their findings with other experts all over the world. The more people work together, the faster they can stop the spread.

Under normal conditions, it can take up to 15 years for scientists to develop a vaccine.

Understanding Viruses

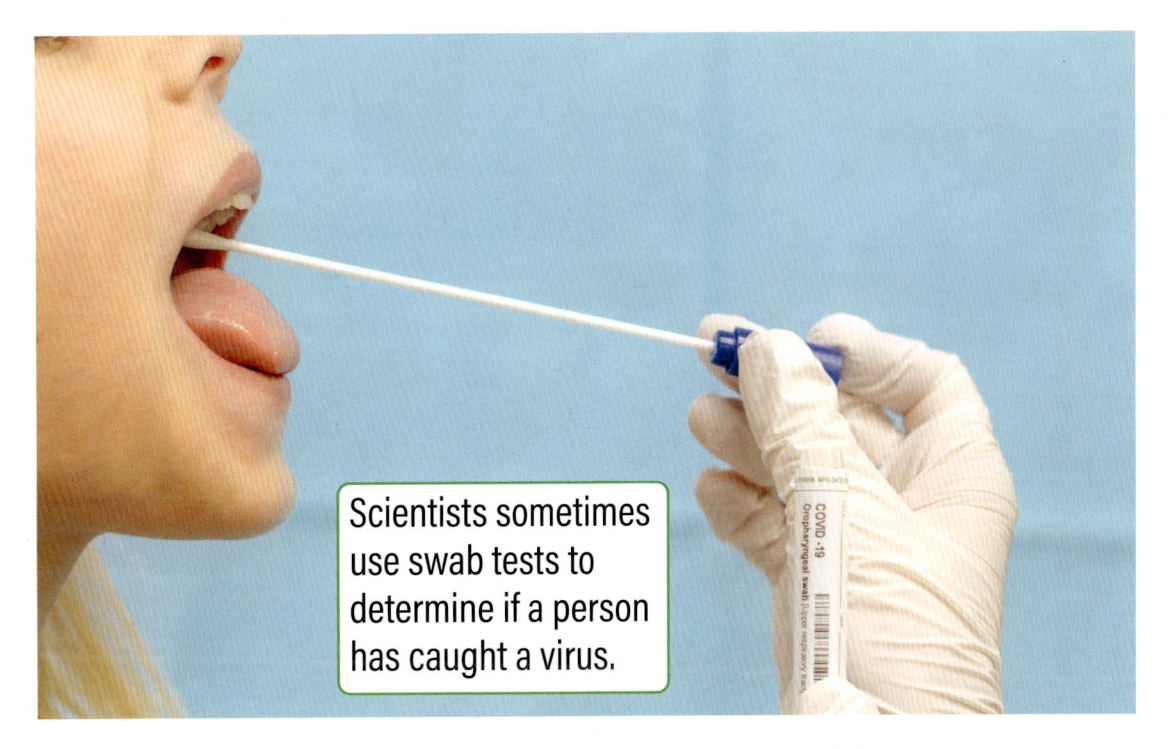

Scientists sometimes use swab tests to determine if a person has caught a virus.

Scientists study a new virus in laboratories. Health workers gather details from infected people. They learn about its signs and symptoms. They try to find out when people first felt sick and for how long. All these details give scientists clues about how to stop the virus.

FAST FACT

In 2015, a person brought a viral disease called Middle East Respiratory Syndrome (MERS) back home to South Korea after a trip to the Middle East. That one person caused an outbreak in South Korea. There were 186 cases and 36 deaths in just two months.

What Is an Epidemic?

Healthcare Heroes

Healthcare plays a big role in epidemics. Many people could get sick during an epidemic. Some may need medicine to get better. They may need to stay in a hospital.

Health workers must protect themselves in an epidemic. They come in contact with many sick people. This means they are more likely to get infected. Health workers must wear masks, gloves, and gowns to keep safe. Many normal health services stop during an epidemic. Health workers must focus on stopping the virus instead. Some people may not be able to go to their doctor for a checkup. Surgeries may be put on hold. Only those who are very sick get the treatments they need.

Countries with a strong health system have many workers and supplies. They are more able to help those who get sick. Poor countries or countries with weak healthcare systems may struggle to help everyone in need. More people may die as a result.

Sometimes, healthcare professionals wear special gear when treating sick patients.

Understanding Viruses

Epidemic Phases

In order to contain an epidemic, government officials and healthcare experts usually follow a series of steps.

PHASE 1 — ANTICIPATE: Experts predict when an epidemic might happen. They plan and prepare.

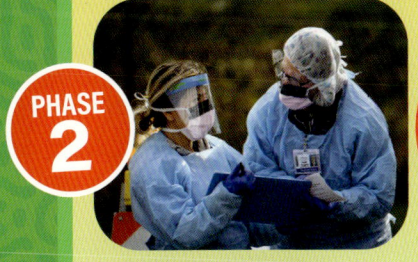

PHASE 2 — DETECT: Health workers learn how to spot signs of an epidemic early.

PHASE 3 — CONTAIN: People take steps to stop the epidemic's spread.

PHASE 4 — CONTROL: Countries and communities try to limit how many people get sick or die.

PHASE 5 — ELIMINATE: Experts find a way to stop the virus from being a threat.

What Is an Epidemic?

Recent Epidemics

There have been many epidemics throughout history. These are a few of the epidemics that have taken place in recent times.

Acquired Immunodeficiency Syndrome (AIDS)
Starting as an epidemic in the Democratic Republic of the Congo, AIDS spreads around the world at this time. By the early 1990s, AIDS has become the leading cause of death in people aged 25 to 44 in the United States.

1950s — **1980s** — **2002** — **2000-2003**

SARS
After its first outbreak in China, the SARS virus spreads around the world. It infects people in 29 countries around the world.

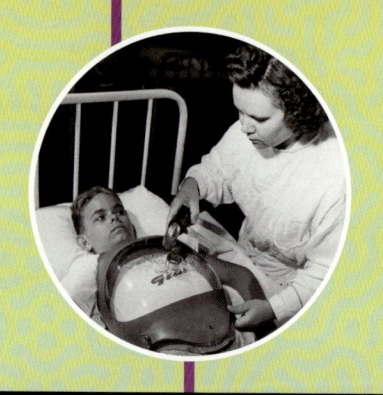

Poliomyelitis
One of the largest polio epidemics in the United States takes place in the 1950s. The disease infects nearly 60,000 children in the country in 1952 alone. About 3,000 die, while thousands are **paralyzed**.

West Nile Virus
More than 4,150 Americans become infected by the West Nile virus. This virus is usually transmitted by infected mosquitoes. The epidemic causes 284 deaths across the United States. Louisiana, Mississippi, and Illinois are badly affected.

18 Understanding Viruses

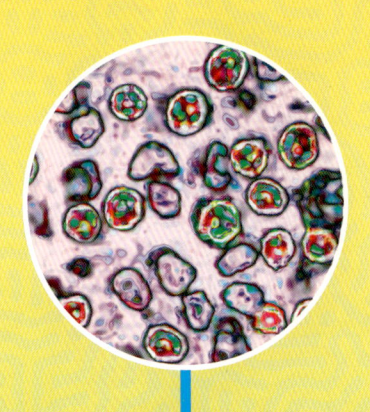

Measles
An outbreak of measles takes place in Quebec, Canada. More than 700 children are infected.

2011

Ebola
The Ebola virus infects more than 28,600 people in West Africa between 2014 and 2016, killing about 11,300. It is the biggest outbreak of the disease ever recorded.

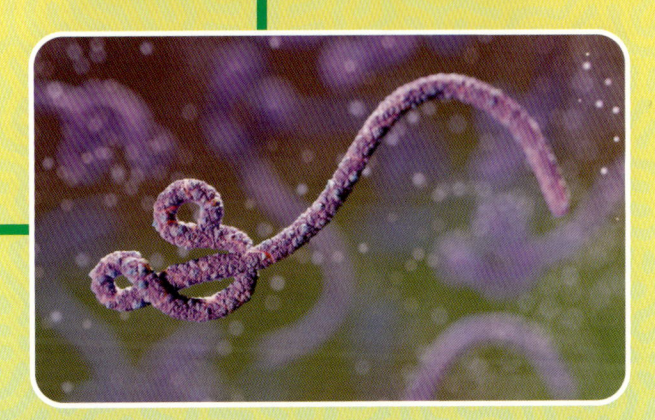

2014–2016

Zika Virus
After various outbreaks in South American and Caribbean countries, Zika virus spreads throughout the Americas. By December 2016, there are more than 700,000 Zika cases in 48 countries and territories in the region.

2015–2016

2019–2020

COVID-19
COVID-19 begins as an outbreak in China in late 2019. By early 2020, it spreads to the rest of the world. The epidemic is officially declared a pandemic on March 11, 2020. The death toll keeps rising as the disease continues to spread.

What Is an Epidemic?

Raising Awareness

Education is one the best ways to stop an epidemic. People can be taught how to spot the signs and symptoms of a particular virus. This way, they can help detect it early. People need to be told what to do if they think they have the virus. They also need to know how to avoid spreading the virus to others. In an epidemic, people may die if they do not do their part. Sharing information can help save lives.

People need to learn how to protect themselves. They cannot help stop the spread if they do not know what to do and why it matters. They are more likely to help if they care about the cause. There are many ways people can get educated about an epidemic. Newspapers and TV news shows are two ways. Medical and government websites are also good places to look for facts. Some communities may put up signs or posters. There may be health phone lines that people can call, too.

During epidemics, people must learn the best ways to protect themselves and reduce the spread of a virus.

ACTIVITY

Make an Epidemic Kit

No one knows when an epidemic will take place, but there are ways people can prepare for one. One way is to build an epidemic kit. It can be hard to buy food and other supplies during an epidemic. Some stores may close. People should limit the number of trips they do make to stores that remain open. This helps stop the spread of the virus. Think about the items your family would need if they could not go to the store. Then, make a list of these items. Be sure to include as many items as possible.

This list shows some examples of items to include in a kit.

Food

Canned fruits and vegetables
Canned meat and fish
Bottled water
Pasta and sauce
Canned soup
Pet food

Supplies

Hand soap and sanitizer
Detergents and disinfectants
Mop and bucket
Paper towels and toilet paper
Can opener

Other Important Items

Medicines
Games and toys
First-aid kit
Face masks and gloves

What Is an Epidemic?

EPIDEMIC QUIZ

1 What is an epidemic?

2 How long does it take to develop a vaccine under normal conditions?

3 Where did the AIDS epidemic first start?

4 How many Americans became infected with West Nile Virus in 2002?

5 Why is it important to detect a virus early?

6 How can people get educated during an epidemic?

7 What do health workers wear to protect themselves?

8 Why do viruses spread more quickly today than in the past?

ANSWERS
1. When a large number of people in the same place get sick at the same time 2. Up to 15 years 3. Democratic Republic of the Congo 4. More than 4,150 5. To help stop its spread 6. Watch the news, read the newspaper, visit government websites and medical websites, look for signs or posters in the community, call health phone lines 7. Gloves, masks, and gowns 8. Airplanes, trains, ships, and cars carry infected people to distant places

Key Words

average: usual or normal level or amount of something
HIV: human immunodeficiency virus, a virus that attacks the body system that fights illness in humans
infected: came in contact with a virus that then entered the system
investigate: to carry out research and find facts
media: newspapers, broadcasts, internet, and other forms of communication
pandemic: a virus that spreads to many parts of the world and affects a large number of people
paralyzed: unable to move
quarantined: kept away from others to stop the spread of a virus
symptoms: body changes that are the consequences of a disease
vaccines: substances made from a small amount of a virus that help build immunity to the virus
virus: a tiny germ that can infect a living being and make it sick

Index

COVID-19 12, 19

disease 4, 6, 7, 15, 18, 19
doctors 8, 10, 16

flu 8, 9

infected 10, 11, 12, 13, 15, 16, 18, 19, 22

measles 8, 19
media 11

outbreak 6, 7, 8, 10, 11, 12, 15, 18, 19, 22

pandemic 7, 19

SARS 4, 5, 18
scientists 4, 6, 7, 10, 11, 13, 14, 15, 22
symptoms 11, 15, 20

vaccines 14

West Nile Virus 18, 22

Get the best of both worlds.

AV2 bridges the gap between print and digital.

The expandable resources toolbar enables quick access to content including **videos**, **audio**, **activities**, **weblinks**, **slideshows**, **quizzes**, and **key words**.

Animated videos make static images come alive.

Resource icons on each page help readers to further **explore key concepts**.

Published by AV2
14 Penn Plaza, 9th Floor
New York, NY 10122
Website: www.av2books.com

Copyright ©2021 AV2
All rights reserved. No part of this publication may be reproduced, stored in a retrieval system, or transmitted in any form or by any means, electronic, mechanical, photocopying, recording, or otherwise, without the prior written permission of the publisher.

Library of Congress Control Number: 2020940994

ISBN 978-1-7911-3247-7 (hardcover)
ISBN 978-1-7911-3246-0 (softcover)
ISBN 978-1-7911-3248-4 (multi-user eBook)
ISBN 978-1-7911-3249-1 (single-user eBook)

Printed in Guangzhou, China
1 2 3 4 5 6 7 8 9 0 24 23 22 21 20

072020
101119

Project Coordinator: Sara Cucini
Designer: Terry Paulhus

Every reasonable effort has been made to trace ownership and to obtain permission to reprint copyright material. The publisher would be pleased to have any errors or omissions brought to their attention so that they may be corrected in subsequent printings.

AV2 acknowledges Getty Images, iStock, and Shutterstock as its primary image suppliers for this title.

View new titles and product videos at www.av2books.com